W9-BSG-719

CROCK·POT.
◆ THE ORIGINAL SLOW COOKER ◆

easy slow cooking

Simple and convenient soups, stews, and more

pil

Publications International, Ltd.

Pictured on the front cover: Beef Barley Soup *(page 114)*.

Pictured on the back cover *(clockwise from top):* BBQ Turkey Legs *(page 30)*, Black Bean Stuffed Peppers *(page 88)* and Ginger Beef with Peppers and Mushrooms *(page 20)*.

ISBN: 978-1-4508-7781-7

Library of Congress Control Number: 2013949165

Manufactured in China.

8 7 6 5 4 3 2 1

Table of Contents

Slow Cooking Hints and Tips

To get the most from your **CROCK-POT**® slow cooker, keep the following hints and tips in mind.

Adding Ingredients at the End of the Cooking Time

Certain ingredients are best added toward the end of the cooking time. These include:

- **Milk, sour cream, and yogurt:** Add during the last 15 minutes.
- **Seafood and fish:** Add during the last 15 to 30 minutes.
- **Fresh herbs:** Fresh herbs such as basil will darken with long cooking, so if you want colorful fresh herbs, add them during the last 15 minutes of cooking or directly to the dish just before serving it.

Pasta and Rice

Converted rice holds up best through slow cooking. If the rice doesn't seem completely cooked after the suggested time, add an extra ½ cup to 1 cup of liquid per cup of rice, and extend the cooking time by 30 to 60 minutes.

Cooking Temperatures and Food Safety

According to the U.S. Department of Agriculture, bacteria in food is killed at a temperature of 165°F. As a result, it's important to follow the recommended cooking times and to keep the cover on your **CROCK-POT**® slow cooker during the cooking process to maintain food-safe temperatures. Slow-cooked meats and poultry are best when simmered gently for the period of time that allows the connective tissues to break down, yielding meat that is fall-off-the-bone tender and juicy.

Browning Meat

Meat will not brown as it would if it were cooked in a skillet or oven at a high temperature. It's not necessary to brown meat before slow cooking. However, if you prefer the look and flavor of browned meat, just brown it in a large skillet sprayed with oil, butter, or nonstick cooking spray, then place the browned ingredients into the stoneware and follow the recipe as written.

Herbs and Spices

When cooking with your **CROCK-POT®** slow cooker, use dried and ground herbs and spices, which work well during long cook times. However, the flavor and aroma of crushed or ground herbs may differ depending on their shelf life, and their flavor can lessen during the extended cooking time in the **CROCK-POT®** slow cooker.

Cooking for Larger Quantity Yields

Follow these guidelines to make a bigger batch in a larger unit, such as a 5-, 6-, or 7-quart **CROCK-POT®** slow cooker:

• Roasted meats, chicken, and turkey quantities may be doubled or tripled, and seasonings adjusted by half. CAUTION: Flavorful dried spices such as garlic or chili powder will intensify during long, slow cooking. Add just 25 to 50 percent more spices, as needed, to balance the flavors.

• When preparing a soup or a stew, you may double all ingredients except the liquids, seasonings, and dried herbs. Increase liquid volume by half, or adjust as needed.

• To avoid over or undercooking, always fill the stoneware ½ to ¾ full and conform to the recommended cooking times (unless instructed otherwise by our **CROCK-POT®** slow cooker recipes).

• Do not double thickeners, such as cornstarch, at the beginning. You may always add more thickener later if it's necessary.

Cooking with Frozen Foods

Slow cooking frozen foods requires a longer cook time than fresh foods because the food needs more time to come up to safe internal temperatures. Meats also will require additional time to allow them to become tender. If there is any question about the cooking time, use a thermometer to ensure meats are cooking appropriately.

Removable Stoneware

The removable stoneware in your **CROCK-POT®** slow cooker makes cleaning easy. However, the stoneware can be damaged by sudden changes in temperature. Here are tips on the use and care of your stoneware:

• Don't preheat the **CROCK-POT®** slow cooker. Don't place cold stoneware into a preheated base.

• Don't place hot stoneware on a cold surface or in the refrigerator; don't fill it with cold water.

• Never place stoneware in the freezer.

• Don't use the stoneware if it's cracked; replace it.

• For further safety tips, please refer to the instruction manual that came with your **CROCK-POT®** slow cooker.

One-Step & Dishes

Mediterranean Chili

2   **cans (about 28 ounces *each*) chickpeas, rinsed and drained**
1   **can (28 ounces) chopped tomatoes**
1   **can (about 14 ounces) vegetable broth**
2   **onions, chopped**
10 **kalamata olives, chopped**
4   **cloves garlic, chopped**
2   **teaspoons ground cumin**
$\frac{1}{4}$ **teaspoon ground red pepper**
$\frac{1}{2}$ **cup chopped fresh mint**
1   **teaspoon dried oregano**
$\frac{1}{2}$ **teaspoon grated lemon peel**
1   **cup crumbled feta cheese**
     Sprigs fresh mint (optional)

Combine chickpeas, tomatoes, broth, onions, olives, garlic, cumin and ground red pepper in **CROCK-POT**® slow cooker. Cover; cook on LOW 7 to 8 hours or on HIGH 3½ hours. Stir in chopped mint, oregano and lemon peel. Top each serving with feta. Garnish with mint sprigs.

Makes 6 servings

One-Step Dishes

Chicken and Rice

3	cans (10¾ ounces *each*) condensed cream of chicken soup, undiluted
2	cups uncooked instant rice
1	cup water
1	pound boneless, skinless chicken breasts or chicken breast tenders
½	teaspoon salt
¼	teaspoon black pepper
¼	teaspoon paprika
½	cup diced celery

Combine soup, rice and water in **CROCK-POT**® slow cooker. Add chicken; sprinkle with salt, pepper and paprika. Top with celery. Cover; cook on LOW 6 to 8 hours or on HIGH 3 to 4 hours.

Makes 4 servings

Sweet-Sour Cabbage with Apples and Caraway Seeds

4	cups shredded red cabbage
1	large tart apple, peeled, cored and cut crosswise into ¼-inch-thick slices
¼	cup packed light brown sugar
¼	cup water
¼	cup cider vinegar
½	teaspoon salt
¼	teaspoon caraway seeds
	Dash black pepper

Combine cabbage, apple, brown sugar, water, vinegar, salt, caraway seeds and pepper in **CROCK-POT**® slow cooker. Cover; cook on LOW 2½ to 3 hours.

Makes 6 servings

Chicken and Rice

Vegetable Pasta Sauce

2   cans (about 14 ounces *each*) diced tomatoes

1   can (about 14 ounces) whole tomatoes, undrained

1½ cups sliced mushrooms

1   medium red bell pepper, diced

1   medium green bell pepper, diced

1   small yellow squash, cut into ¼-inch slices

1   small zucchini, cut into ¼-inch slices

1   can (6 ounces) tomato paste

4   green onions, sliced

2   tablespoons Italian seasoning

1   tablespoon chopped fresh Italian parsley

3   cloves garlic, minced

1   teaspoon salt

1   teaspoon red pepper flakes (optional)

1   teaspoon black pepper

     Hot cooked pasta

     Grated Parmesan cheese (optional)

Combine tomatoes, mushrooms, bell peppers, squash, zucchini, tomato paste, green onions, Italian seasoning, parsley, garlic, salt, red pepper flakes, if desired, and black pepper in **CROCK-POT**® slow cooker; stir until well blended. Cover; cook on LOW 6 to 8 hours. Serve over pasta. Top with Parmesan cheese, if desired.

Makes 4 to 6 servings

One-Step Dishes

Pork in Chile Sauce

2   **cups tomato purée**

2   **large tomatoes, chopped**

2   **small poblano peppers, seeded and chopped**

2   **large shallots *or* 1 small onion, chopped**

2   **cloves garlic, minced**

½   **teaspoon dried oregano**

¼   **teaspoon chipotle chili powder or regular chili powder***

¼   **teaspoon black pepper**

2   **(6-ounce) boneless pork chops, cut into 1-inch pieces**

4   **whole wheat or corn tortillas, warmed**

*Chipotle chili powder is available in the spice section of most supermarkets.

Place tomato purée, tomatoes, poblano peppers, shallots, garlic, oregano, chili powder and black pepper in **CROCK-POT**® slow cooker; mix well. Add pork. Cover; cook on LOW 5 to 6 hours. Serve in tortillas.

Makes 4 servings

Pork Roast with Dijon Tarragon Glaze

1½ to 2	pounds boneless pork loin, trimmed
1	teaspoon ground paprika
½	teaspoon black pepper
⅓	cup chicken or vegetable broth
2	tablespoons Dijon mustard
2	tablespoons lemon juice
1	teaspoon minced fresh tarragon

Sprinkle pork with paprika and pepper. Place roast in **CROCK-POT**® slow cooker. Combine broth, mustard, lemon juice and tarragon in small bowl; spoon over roast. Cover; cook on LOW 6 to 8 hours or on HIGH 3 to 4 hours. Remove roast to cutting board. Cover loosely with foil; let stand 10 to 15 minutes before slicing. Serve with cooking liquid.

Makes 4 to 6 servings

Cashew Chicken

6	boneless, skinless chicken breasts
1½	cups cashew nuts
1	cup sliced mushrooms
1	cup sliced celery
1	can (10¾ ounces) condensed cream of mushroom soup, undiluted
¼	cup chopped green onions
2	tablespoons butter
1½	tablespoons soy sauce
	Hot cooked rice

Combine chicken, cashews, mushrooms, celery, soup, green onions, butter and soy sauce in **CROCK-POT**® slow cooker. Cover; cook on LOW 6 to 8 hours or on HIGH 4 to 6 hours. Serve over rice.

Makes 6 servings

Pork Roast with Dijon Tarragon Glaze

One-Step Dishes

Mushroom Wild Rice

1½ cups chicken broth

1 cup uncooked wild rice

½ cup diced onion

½ cup sliced mushrooms

½ cup diced red or green bell pepper

1 tablespoon olive oil

¼ teaspoon salt

¼ teaspoon black pepper

Place broth, rice, onion, mushrooms, bell pepper, oil, salt and black pepper in **CROCK-POT®** slow cooker. Cover; cook on HIGH 2½ hours or until rice is tender and liquid is absorbed.

Makes 8 servings

Tip: Wild rice should be thoroughly rinsed before cooking to remove any debris remaining from processing. To rinse, place raw rice in a medium bowl with cold water, stir and allow it to sit until the debris floats to the surface. Remove the debris and drain.

One-Step Dishes

3-Cheese Chicken and Noodles

3	cups chopped cooked chicken
1½	cups cottage cheese
1	can (10¾ ounces) condensed cream of chicken soup, undiluted
1	package (8 ounces) wide egg noodles, cooked and drained
1	cup (4 ounces) shredded Monterey Jack cheese
½	cup grated Parmesan cheese
½	cup diced onion
½	cup diced celery
½	cup diced green bell pepper
½	cup diced red bell pepper
½	cup chicken broth
1	can (4 ounces) sliced mushrooms, drained
2	tablespoons butter, melted
½	teaspoon dried thyme
	Crusty rolls and asparagus (optional)

Combine chicken, cottage cheese, soup, noodles, cheeses, onion, celery, bell peppers, broth, mushrooms, butter and thyme in **CROCK-POT**® slow cooker; stir to blend. Cover; cook on LOW 6 to 8 hours or on HIGH 3 to 4 hours. Serve with rolls and asparagus, if desired.

Makes 6 servings

Ginger Beef with Peppers and Mushrooms

1½	pounds boneless beef top round steak, cut into ¾-inch cubes
24	baby carrots
1	onion, chopped
1	red bell pepper, chopped
1	green bell pepper, chopped
1	package (8 ounces) mushrooms, cut into halves
1	cup beef broth
½	cup hoisin sauce
¼	cup quick-cooking tapioca
2	tablespoons grated fresh ginger
	Hot cooked rice

Combine beef, carrots, onion, bell peppers, mushrooms, broth, hoisin sauce, tapioca and ginger in **CROCK-POT**® slow cooker. Cover; cook on LOW 8 to 9 hours. Serve over rice.

Makes 6 servings

Tip: Boneless beef top round steak can also sometimes be found in the meat section packaged as London Broil. Both are the same cut of beef, however, London Broil is thicker.

Cinnamon Roll-Topped Mixed Berry Cobbler

2 bags (12 ounces *each*) frozen mixed berries, thawed

1 cup sugar

¼ cup quick-cooking tapioca

¼ cup water

2 teaspoons vanilla

1 package (about 12 ounces) refrigerated cinnamon rolls with icing

Stir berries, sugar, tapioca, water and vanilla into 4-quart **CROCK-POT®** slow cooker; top with cinnamon rolls. Cover; cook on LOW 4 to 5 hours. Serve warm, drizzled with icing.

Makes 8 servings

4-Fruit Oatmeal

4¼ cups water

1 cup steel-cut oats

⅓ cup golden raisins

⅓ cup dried cranberries

⅓ cup dried cherries

2 tablespoons honey

1 teaspoon vanilla

¼ teaspoon salt

1 cup sliced fresh strawberries

Combine water, oats, raisins, cranberries, cherries, honey, vanilla and salt in **CROCK-POT®** slow cooker; stir well. Cover; cook on LOW 7 to 7½ hours. Top each serving evenly with strawberries.

Makes 4 servings

Cinnamon Roll-Topped
Mixed Berry Cobbler

Kielbasa and Cabbage

2　pounds kielbasa, cut into ¾-inch-thick pieces

2　pounds small red potatoes, quartered

1　pound cabbage, shredded

1　large onion, coarsely chopped

¼　cup chicken broth

4　cloves garlic, minced

2　teaspoons fennel seed

1　teaspoon caraway seeds

¼　teaspoon black pepper

Place kielbasa, potatoes, cabbage, onion, broth, garlic, fennel seed, caraway seeds and pepper in **CROCK-POT**® slow cooker. Cover; cook on HIGH 4 to 5 hours or until potatoes are fork-tender and cabbage is crisp-tender.

Makes 6 servings

Tip: Kielbasa or polish sausage has a garlic flavor and consists mainly of seasoned pork, although beef and veal are often added. It is commonly sold in long links that are smoked and precooked. The links are ready to heat and serve.

Spinach, Crab and Artichoke Dip

1   can (6½ ounces) crabmeat, drained and shredded

1   package (10 ounces) frozen chopped spinach, thawed and squeezed nearly dry

1   package (8 ounces) cream cheese

1   jar (about 6 ounces) marinated artichoke hearts, drained and finely chopped

¼   teaspoon hot pepper sauce

     Melba toast or whole grain crackers (optional)

Pick out and discard any shell or cartilage from crabmeat. Combine crabmeat, spinach, cream cheese, artichokes and hot pepper sauce in 1½-quart **CROCK-POT**® slow cooker. Cover; cook on HIGH 1½ to 2 hours or until heated through, stirring after 1 hour. Serve with melba toast, if desired.

Makes 10 servings

Apricot and Brie Dip

½   cup dried apricots, finely chopped

⅓   cup plus 1 tablespoon apricot preserves, divided

¼   cup apple juice

1   round wheel Brie cheese (2 pounds), rind removed and cut into cubes

     Bread or crackers (optional)

Combine dried apricots, ⅓ cup apricot preserves and apple juice in **CROCK-POT**® slow cooker. Cover; cook on HIGH 40 minutes. Stir in cheese. Cover; cook on HIGH 30 to 40 minutes or until cheese is melted. Stir in remaining 1 tablespoon preserves. Turn **CROCK-POT**® slow cooker to LOW. Serve warm with bread, if desired.

Makes 3 cups

Spinach, Crab and Artichoke Dip

4 Ingredients or Less

Fantastic Pot Roast

- 1 **can (12 ounces) cola**
- 1 **bottle (10 ounces) chili sauce**
- 2 **cloves garlic (optional)**
- 2½ **pounds boneless beef chuck roast**
  Fresh cooked green beans (optional)

Combine cola, chili sauce and garlic, if desired, in **CROCK-POT**® slow cooker. Add beef; turn to coat. Cover; cook on LOW 6 to 8 hours. Serve with sauce and green beans, if desired.

Makes 6 servings

BBQ Turkey Legs

6   **turkey drumsticks**
2   **teaspoons salt**
2   **teaspoons black pepper**
2   **cups prepared barbecue sauce**

Season drumsticks with salt and pepper. Place in **CROCK-POT**® slow cooker. Add barbecue sauce; turn to coat. Cover; cook on LOW 7 to 8 hours or on HIGH 3 to 4 hours.

Makes 6 servings

Easy Family Burritos

1   **boneless beef chuck shoulder roast (2 to 3 pounds)***
1   **jar (24 ounces)** *or* **2 jars (16 ounces** *each***) salsa**
     Flour tortillas, warmed
     Optional toppings: shredded cheese, sour cream, salsa, shredded lettuce, diced tomato, diced onion and/or guacamole

*Unless you have a 5-, 6- or 7-quart **CROCK-POT**® slow cooker, cut any roast larger than 2½ pounds in half so it cooks completely.*

1. Place beef in **CROCK-POT**® slow cooker; top with salsa. Cover; cook on LOW 8 to 10 hours.

2. Remove beef to cutting board; shred with two forks. Return to cooking liquid; mix well. Cover; cook on LOW 1 to 2 hours or until heated through. Serve beef in tortillas. Top as desired.

Makes 8 servings

BBQ Turkey Legs

Slow Cooker Turkey Breast

½   **to 1 teaspoon garlic powder**
½   **to 1 teaspoon paprika**
1   **turkey breast (4 to 6 pounds)**
1   **tablespoon dried parsley flakes**

1. Combine garlic powder and paprika in small bowl; rub onto turkey. Place turkey in **CROCK-POT®** slow cooker. Sprinkle with parsley flakes. Cover; cook on LOW 6 to 8 hours or on HIGH 2½ to 3 hours or until cooked through.

2. Remove turkey to cutting board. Cover loosely with foil; let stand 10 to 15 minutes before slicing.

Makes 4 to 6 servings

Chicken and Biscuits

4   **boneless, skinless chicken breasts, cut into 1-inch pieces**
1   **can (10¾ ounces) condensed cream of chicken soup**
1   **package (10 ounces) frozen peas and carrots, thawed**
1   **package (7½ ounces) refrigerated biscuits**

1. Place chicken in **CROCK-POT®** slow cooker; pour in soup. Cover; cook on LOW 4 hours or until chicken is cooked through.

2. Stir in peas and carrots. Cover; cook on LOW 30 minutes or until vegetables are heated through.

3. Meanwhile, bake biscuits according to package directions. Spoon chicken and vegetable mixture over biscuits to serve.

Makes 4 servings

**Slow Cooker
Turkey Breast**

Italian Beef

1	beef rump roast (3 to 5 pounds)*
1	can (about 14 ounces) beef broth
2	cups mild giardiniera
8	crusty Italian bread rolls, split

*Unless you have a 5-, 6- or 7-quart **CROCK-POT**® slow cooker, cut any roast larger than 2½ pounds in half so it cooks completely.*

1. Place beef in **CROCK-POT**® slow cooker; add broth and giardiniera. Cover; cook on LOW 10 hours.

2. Remove beef to cutting board; shred with two forks. Return to cooking liquid; mix well. To serve, spoon beef and sauce onto rolls.

Makes 8 servings

Salsa-Style Wings

2	tablespoons oil
1½	pounds chicken wings (18 wings)
2	cups salsa
¼	cup packed brown sugar

1. Heat oil in large skillet over medium-high heat. Add wings in batches; cook 3 to 4 minutes or until wings are browned on all sides. Remove to **CROCK-POT**® slow cooker. Combine salsa and brown sugar in medium bowl; stir until well blended. Pour over chicken.

2. Cover; cook on LOW 5 to 6 hours or on HIGH 2 to 3 hours. Serve wings with salsa mixture.

Makes 18 wings

Italian Beef

4 Ingredients or Less

Posole

3 **pounds pork tenderloin, cubed**

3 **cans (about 14 ounces *each*) white hominy, rinsed and drained**

1 **cup chili sauce**

Combine pork, hominy and chili sauce in **CROCK-POT**® slow cooker. Cover; cook on LOW 10 hours or on HIGH 5 hours.

Makes 8 servings

Glazed Pork Loin

1 **bag (1 pound) baby carrots**

4 **boneless pork loin chops**

1 **jar (8 ounces) apricot preserves**

Place carrots on bottom of **CROCK-POT**® slow cooker. Place pork on top; spread with preserves. Cover; cook on LOW 8 hours or on HIGH 4 hours.

Makes 4 servings

Posole

4 Ingredients or Less

Carne Rellenos

1   can (4 ounces) whole mild green chiles, drained
4   ounces cream cheese, softened
1   flank steak (about 2 pounds)
1½ cups salsa verde
     Hot cooked rice (optional)

1. Slit whole chiles open on one side with sharp knife; stuff with cream cheese.

2. Open steak flat on sheet of waxed paper. Score steak; turn over. Lay stuffed chiles across unscored side of steak. Roll up; tie with kitchen string.

3. Place steak in **CROCK-POT**® slow cooker; pour in salsa. Cover; cook on LOW 6 to 8 hours or on HIGH 3 to 4 hours or until cooked through. Remove steak to cutting board; slice. Serve over rice with sauce, if desired.

Makes 6 servings

Hot and Sour Chicken

4   to 6 boneless, skinless chicken breasts (1 to 1½ pounds total)
1   cup chicken or vegetable broth
1   package (about 1 ounce) dry hot-and-sour soup mix
     Sugar snap peas and diced red bell pepper (optional)

Place chicken in **CROCK-POT**® slow cooker; add broth and soup mix. Cover; cook on LOW 5 to 6 hours. Serve chicken over peas and bell pepper, if desired.

Makes 4 to 6 servings

Carne Rellenos

Barbecue Roast Beef

2 **pounds cooked boneless roast beef**

1 **bottle (12 ounces) barbecue sauce**

1½ **cups water**

10 **to 12 sandwich rolls, split**

1. Combine roast beef, barbecue sauce and water in **CROCK-POT**® slow cooker. Cover; cook on LOW 2 hours.

2. Remove beef to cutting board; shred with two forks. Return beef to sauce; mix well. Serve on rolls.

Makes 10 to 12 servings

Tip: To save time, freeze leftovers as individual portions. Just reheat in a microwave for fast meals!

Easy Cheesy BBQ Chicken

6	**boneless, skinless chicken breasts (about 1½ pounds)**
1	**bottle (26 ounces) barbecue sauce**
6	**slices bacon, crisp-cooked and cut in half**
6	**slices Swiss cheese**

1. Place chicken in **CROCK-POT**® slow cooker; pour in barbecue sauce. Cover; cook on LOW 8 to 9 hours. (If sauce becomes too thick during cooking, add a little water.)

2. Place 2 bacon halves and 1 cheese slice on each chicken breast in **CROCK-POT**® slow cooker. Turn **CROCK-POT**® slow cooker to HIGH. Cover; cook on HIGH 15 minutes or until cheese is melted.

Makes 6 servings

Tip: To make cleanup easier, coat the inside of the **CROCK-POT**® slow cooker with nonstick cooking spray before adding the ingredients. To remove any sticky barbecue sauce residue, soak the stoneware in hot sudsy water, then scrub it with a plastic or nylon scrubber. Don't use steel wool.

Harvest Ham Supper

6   **carrots, cut into 2-inch pieces**
3   **medium sweet potatoes, quartered**
1   **to 1½ pounds boneless ham**
1   **cup maple syrup**

1. Arrange carrots and sweet potatoes in bottom of **CROCK-POT**® slow cooker.

2. Place ham on top of vegetables. Pour syrup over ham and vegetables. Cover; cook on LOW 6 to 8 hours.

Makes 6 servings

Spicy Shredded Chicken

6   **boneless, skinless chicken breasts (about 1½ pounds)**
1   **jar (16 ounces) salsa**
     Flour tortillas, warmed
     Optional toppings: shredded cheese, sour cream, shredded lettuce, diced tomato, diced onion and/or sliced avocado

1. Place chicken in **CROCK-POT**® slow cooker; top with salsa. Cover; cook on LOW 6 to 8 hours or until chicken is cooked through.

2. Remove chicken to cutting board; shred with two forks. Serve in warmed tortillas. Top as desired.

Makes 6 servings

Harvest Ham Supper

Triple Chocolate Fantasy

2 **pounds white almond bark, broken into pieces**

1 **bar (4 ounces) sweetened chocolate, broken into pieces***

1 **package (12 ounces) semisweet chocolate chips**

3 **cups coarsely chopped pecans, lightly toasted****

*Use your favorite high-quality chocolate candy bar.

**To toast pecans, spread in single layer in heavy skillet. Cook and stir over medium heat 1 to 2 minutes or until nuts are lightly browned.

1. Place bark, sweetened chocolate and chocolate chips in **CROCK-POT**® slow cooker. Cover; cook on HIGH 1 hour. Do not stir.

2. Turn **CROCK-POT**® slow cooker to LOW. Cover; cook on LOW 1 hour, stirring every 15 minutes. Stir in nuts.

3. Drop mixture by tablespoonfuls onto baking sheet covered with waxed paper; cool. Store in tightly covered container.

Makes 36 pieces

Variations: Here are a few ideas for other imaginative items to add in along with or instead of the pecans: raisins, crushed peppermint candy, candy-coated baking bits, crushed toffee, peanuts or pistachio nuts, chopped gum drops, chopped dried fruit, candied cherries, chopped marshmallows or sweetened coconut.

Red Hot Applesauce

10   to 12 apples, peeled, cored and chopped
¾   cup hot cinnamon candies
½   cup apple juice or water
     Lemon peel twist (optional)
     Sprig fresh mint (optional)

Combine apples, candies and apple juice in **CROCK-POT**® slow cooker. Cover; cook on LOW 7 to 8 hours or on HIGH 4 hours or until desired consistency. Garnish with lemon twist and mint.

Makes 6 servings

Spicy Sweet and Sour Cocktail Franks

2   packages (8 ounces *each*) cocktail franks
½   cup ketchup or chili sauce
½   cup apricot preserves
1   teaspoon hot pepper sauce

Combine cocktail franks, ketchup, preserves and hot pepper sauce in 1½-quart **CROCK-POT**® slow cooker; mix well. Cover; cook on LOW 2 to 3 hours.

Makes 10 to 12 servings

Red Hot Applesauce

Family & Favorites

Cheeseburger Sloppy Joes

- 1½ **pounds ground beef**
- 3 **cloves garlic, minced**
- 1 **small onion, finely chopped (about ½ cup)**
- ½ **cup ketchup**
- ¼ **cup water**
- 1 **tablespoon packed brown sugar**
- 1 **teaspoon Worcestershire sauce**
- 2 **cups (8 ounces) shredded sharp Cheddar cheese**
- 6 **to 8 hamburger rolls**

1. Coat inside of **CROCK-POT**® slow cooker with nonstick cooking spray. Brown beef in large nonstick skillet over medium-high heat 6 to 8 minutes, stirring to break up meat. Drain fat. Stir in garlic and onion; cook and stir 3 to 4 minutes.

2. Add beef mixture, ketchup, water, brown sugar and Worcestershire sauce to **CROCK-POT**® slow cooker; stir to blend. Cover; cook on LOW 4 to 5 hours or on HIGH 2 to 2½ hours. Stir in cheese until melted. Divide evenly among rolls.

Makes 6 to 8 servings

Spaghetti and Turkey Meatballs

1½ **pounds ground turkey**
½ **cup Italian seasoned dry bread crumbs**
1 **small onion, finely chopped**
2 **teaspoons garlic powder, divided**
2 **eggs**
½ **cup grated Parmesan cheese**
½ **teaspoon black pepper, divided**
2 **tablespoons olive oil**
1 **can (28 ounces) crushed tomatoes with basil, oregano and garlic**
1 **can (6 ounces) tomato paste**
1 **teaspoon dried basil**
   Hot cooked spaghetti
   Chopped fresh Italian parsley (optional)

1. Coat inside of **CROCK-POT**® slow cooker with nonstick cooking spray. Combine turkey, bread crumbs, onion, 1 teaspoon garlic powder, eggs, cheese and ¼ teaspoon pepper in large bowl; mix well. Form mixture into 24 meatballs, about 1½ inches in diameter. Heat oil in large skillet over medium-high heat. Add meatballs in batches; cook and stir 4 to 5 minutes or until browned on all sides. Remove meatballs to **CROCK-POT**® slow cooker using slotted spoon.

2. Combine tomatoes, tomato paste and basil in large bowl; stir to blend. Pour over meatballs. Cover; cook on LOW 6 to 7 hours or on HIGH 3 to 4 hours or until meatballs are cooked through. Serve over spaghetti. Garnish with parsley.

Makes 6 servings

Ravioli Casserole

8	ounces pork or turkey Italian sausage, casings removed
½	cup minced onion
1½	cups marinara sauce
1	can (about 14 ounces) Italian-style diced tomatoes
2	packages (9 ounces *each*) refrigerated meatless ravioli, such as wild mushroom or three cheese, divided
1½	cups (6 ounces) shredded mozzarella cheese, divided
	Chopped fresh Italian parsley (optional)

1. Heat large skillet over medium-high heat. Brown sausage and onion 6 to 8 minutes, stirring to break up meat. Drain fat. Stir in marinara sauce and tomatoes; mix well. Remove from heat.

2. Coat inside of **CROCK-POT**® slow cooker with nonstick cooking spray. Spoon 1 cup sauce into **CROCK-POT**® slow cooker. Layer half of 1 package of ravioli over sauce; top with additional ½ cup sauce. Repeat layering once; top with ½ cup cheese. Repeat layering with remaining package ravioli and all remaining sauce, reserve remaining ½ cup cheese. Cover; cook on LOW 2½ to 3 hours or on HIGH 1½ to 2 hours or until sauce is heated through and ravioli is tender.

3. Sprinkle remaining ½ cup cheese over top of casserole. Cover; cook on HIGH 15 minutes or until cheese is melted. Garnish with parsley.

Makes 4 to 6 servings

Southwest-Style Meat Loaf

1½ **pounds ground beef**

2 **eggs**

1 **small onion, chopped (about ½ cup)**

½ **medium green bell pepper, chopped (about ½ cup)**

½ **cup plain dry bread crumbs**

¾ **cup chunky salsa, divided**

1½ **teaspoons ground cumin**

¾ **cup (3 ounces) shredded Mexican cheese blend**

¾ **teaspoon salt**

¼ **teaspoon black pepper**

1. Combine beef, eggs, onion, bell pepper, bread crumbs, ¼ cup salsa, cumin, cheese, salt and black pepper in large bowl; mix well. Form mixture into 9 × 5-inch loaf.

2. Fold two long pieces of foil in half lengthwise. (Each should be about 24 inches long.) Crisscross pieces on work surface, coat with nonstick cooking spray and set meat loaf on top. Use ends of foil as handles to gently lower meat loaf into **CROCK-POT**® slow cooker, letting ends hang over the top. Top meat loaf with remaining ½ cup salsa.

3. Cover; cook on LOW 7 to 8 hours or on HIGH 3 to 4 hours or until meat loaf is firm and cooked through. Remove meat loaf to cutting board; let stand 5 minutes before slicing.

Makes 6 servings

Pizza-Style Mostaccioli

1	jar (24 to 26 ounces) marinara sauce or tomato basil pasta sauce
½	cup water
2	cups (6 ounces) uncooked mostaccioli pasta
1	package (8 ounces) sliced mushrooms
1	small yellow or green bell pepper, finely diced
½	cup (1 ounce) sliced pepperoni, halved
1	teaspoon dried oregano
¼	teaspoon red pepper flakes
1	cup (4 ounces) shredded pizza cheese blend or Italian cheese blend
	Chopped fresh oregano (optional)
	Garlic bread (optional)

1. Coat inside of **CROCK-POT**® slow cooker with nonstick cooking spray. Combine marinara sauce and water in **CROCK-POT**® slow cooker. Stir in pasta, mushrooms, bell pepper, pepperoni, dried oregano and red pepper flakes; mix well. Cover; cook on LOW 2 hours or on HIGH 1 hour.

2. Stir well.* Cover; cook on LOW 1½ to 2 hours or on HIGH 45 minutes to 1 hour or until pasta and vegetables are tender. Spoon into shallow bowls. Top with cheese and garnish with fresh oregano. Serve with bread, if desired.

Makes 4 servings

Stirring halfway through cooking time prevents the pasta on the bottom from becoming overcooked.

Homestyle Mac 'n' Cheese

12   ounces uncooked elbow macaroni (about 3 cups)
2   cans (12 ounce *each*) evaporated milk
1   cup milk
⅓   cup all-purpose flour
¼   cup (½ stick) unsalted butter, melted
2   eggs, lightly beaten
1   teaspoon dry mustard
½   teaspoon salt
¼   teaspoon black pepper
4   cups (16 ounces) shredded sharp Cheddar cheese
    Toasted bread crumbs (optional)

1. Coat inside of **CROCK-POT**® slow cooker with nonstick cooking spray. Bring large saucepan of lightly salted water to a boil. Add macaroni; cook according to package directions; drain. Remove to **CROCK-POT**® slow cooker.

2. Combine evaporated milk, milk, flour, butter, eggs, dry mustard, salt and pepper in large bowl; add to **CROCK-POT**® slow cooker. Stir in cheese until well combined.

3. Cover; cook on LOW 3½ to 4 hours or until cheese is melted and macaroni is tender. Stir well. Top each serving with bread crumbs, if desired.

Makes 6 to 8 servings

Slow Cooker Pizza Casserole

1½ pounds ground beef

1 pound bulk pork sausage

4 jars (14 ounces *each*) pizza sauce

2 cups (8 ounces) shredded mozzarella cheese

2 cups grated Parmesan cheese

2 cans (4 ounces *each*) mushroom stems and pieces, drained

2 packages (3 ounces *each*) sliced pepperoni

½ cup finely chopped onion

½ cup finely chopped green bell pepper

1 clove garlic, minced

1 pound corkscrew pasta, cooked and drained

1. Brown beef and sausage in large nonstick skillet over medium-high heat 6 to 8 minutes, stirring to break up meat. Drain fat. Remove beef mixture to **CROCK-POT®** slow cooker using slotted spoon.

2. Add pizza sauce, cheeses, mushrooms, pepperoni, onion, bell pepper and garlic; stir to blend. Cover; cook on LOW 3½ hours or on HIGH 2 hours.

3. Stir in pasta. Cover; cook on HIGH 15 to 20 minutes or until pasta is heated through.

Makes 6 servings

Boneless Chicken Cacciatore

Olive oil

6	boneless, skinless chicken breasts, sliced in half horizontally
4	cups tomato-basil pasta sauce
1	cup coarsely chopped yellow onion
1	cup coarsely chopped green bell pepper
1	can (6 ounces) sliced mushrooms
¼	cup dry red wine (optional)
2	teaspoons minced garlic
2	teaspoons dried oregano
2	teaspoons dried thyme
2	teaspoons salt
2	teaspoons black pepper

Hot cooked pasta

1. Heat oil in large skillet over medium heat. Add chicken; cook 6 to 8 minutes or until browned on both sides. Remove to **CROCK-POT**® slow cooker.

2. Add pasta sauce, onion, bell pepper, mushrooms, wine, if desired, garlic, oregano, thyme, salt and black pepper to **CROCK-POT**® slow cooker; stir to blend. Cover; cook on LOW 5 to 7 hours or on HIGH 2 to 3 hours. Serve over pasta.

Makes 6 servings

Ham and Potato Casserole

1½ pounds red potatoes, sliced

8 ounces thinly sliced ham

2 poblano peppers, cut into thin strips

2 tablespoons olive oil

1 tablespoon dried oregano

¼ teaspoon salt

1 cup (4 ounces) shredded Monterey Jack or pepper jack cheese

2 tablespoons finely chopped fresh cilantro

1. Combine potatoes, ham, poblano peppers, oil and oregano in **CROCK-POT®** slow cooker; stir to blend. Cover; cook on LOW 7 hours or on HIGH 4 hours.

2. Remove to large serving platter; sprinkle with cheese and cilantro. Let stand 3 minutes or until cheese is melted.

Makes 6 to 7 servings

Tip: Poblano peppers are very dark green, large triangular-shaped chiles with pointed ends. They are usually 3 to 5 inches long and their flavor ranges from mild to quite hot.

Hearty Chili Mac

1	**pound ground beef**
1	**can (about 14 ounces) diced tomatoes, drained**
1	**cup chopped onion**
1	**tablespoon chili powder**
1	**clove garlic, minced**
½	**teaspoon salt**
½	**teaspoon ground cumin**
½	**teaspoon dried oregano**
¼	**teaspoon red pepper flakes**
¼	**teaspoon black pepper**
2	**cups hot cooked elbow macaroni**

1. Brown beef in large skillet over medium-high heat 6 to 8 minutes, stirring to break up meat. Drain fat. Remove to **CROCK-POT**® slow cooker.

2. Add tomatoes, onion, chili powder, garlic, salt, cumin, oregano, red pepper flakes and black pepper to **CROCK-POT**® slow cooker; mix well. Cover; cook on LOW 4 hours.

3. Stir in macaroni. Cover; cook on LOW 1 hour.

Makes 4 servings

Sticky Caramel Pumpkin Cake

2	cups all-purpose flour
2	teaspoons baking powder
1	teaspoon baking soda
½	teaspoon salt
½	teaspoon pumpkin pie spice or ground cinnamon
1⅓	cups sugar
1	cup (2 sticks) unsalted butter, softened
4	eggs, at room temperature
1	can (15 ounces) solid-pack pumpkin
1	jar (16 ounces) caramel sauce or caramel ice cream topping, divided
	Vanilla ice cream (optional)

1. Coat inside of 4½-quart **CROCK-POT**® slow cooker with nonstick cooking spray.

2. Combine flour, baking powder, baking soda, salt and pumpkin pie spice in large bowl. Beat sugar and butter in separate large bowl with electric mixer at high speed 3 minutes or until blended. Add eggs, one at a time, beating well after each addition. Beat in pumpkin. Beat in flour mixture at low speed until smooth. Spread evenly in **CROCK-POT**® slow cooker.

3. Cover; cook on HIGH 2 to 2½ hours or until toothpick inserted into center of cake comes out clean. Drizzle ½ cup caramel sauce over cake. Serve warm with ice cream. Drizzle with additional caramel sauce.

Makes 8 servings

Serving Suggestion: For a fancier presentation, trim a sheet of waxed paper to fit the bottom of the stoneware. Spray the stoneware and waxed paper with nonstick cooking spray. Proceed as directed above, but before drizzling with caramel sauce, place a large plate upside-down on top of the Sticky Caramel Pumpkin Cake and invert the stoneware allowing the cake to slide out onto the plate. Peel waxed paper from bottom of cake, then invert onto large serving plate.

Comforting Classics

Barbecue Ribs

	Canola oil or vegetable oil
2	small red onions, finely chopped
3	to 4 cloves garlic, minced
1	cup packed brown sugar
1	cup ketchup
½	cup cider vinegar
	Juice of 1 lemon
2	tablespoons Worcestershire sauce
1	tablespoon hot pepper sauce
½	teaspoon chili powder
2	racks pork baby back ribs, cut into 3- to 4-rib sections

1. Heat oil in large skillet over medium heat. Add onions and garlic; cook and stir 3 to 5 minutes or until softened and lightly browned. Stir in brown sugar, ketchup, vinegar, lemon juice, Worcestershire sauce, hot pepper sauce and chili powder; cook and stir 5 minutes. Remove half of sauce and reserve.

2. Remove remaining sauce to **CROCK-POT**® slow cooker. Add ribs; turn to coat. Cover; cook on LOW 7 to 9 hours or on HIGH 4 to 6 hours. Serve ribs with reserved sauce.

Makes 6 servings

Corn on the Cob with Garlic Herb Butter

½   **cup (1 stick) unsalted butter, softened**

3   **to 4 cloves garlic, minced**

2   **tablespoons finely minced fresh Italian parsley**

4   **to 5 ears of corn, husked**

    Salt and black pepper

1. Place each ear of corn on a piece of foil. Combine butter, garlic and parsley in small bowl; spread onto corn. Season with salt and pepper; tightly seal foil.

2. Place in **CROCK-POT**® slow cooker, overlapping ears, if necessary. Add enough water to come one fourth of the way up each ear. Cover; cook on LOW 4 to 5 hours or on HIGH 2 to 2½ hours.

Makes 4 to 5 servings

Scalloped Potatoes and Ham

6   **large russet potatoes, sliced into ¼-inch rounds**

1   **ham steak (about 1½ pounds), cut into cubes**

1   **can (10½ ounces) condensed cream of mushroom soup, undiluted**

1   **soup can water**

1   **cup (4 ounces) shredded Cheddar cheese**

1. Coat inside of **CROCK-POT**® slow cooker with nonstick cooking spray. Arrange potatoes and ham in layers in **CROCK-POT**® slow cooker.

2. Combine soup, water and cheese in medium bowl; pour over potatoes and ham. Cover; cook on HIGH 3½ hours or until potatoes are tender. Turn **CROCK-POT**® slow cooker to LOW. Cover; cook on LOW 1 hour.

Makes 5 to 6 servings

**Corn on the Cob
with Garlic Herb Butter**

Slow Cooker Meat Loaf

1½	pounds ground beef
¾	cup milk
⅔	cup fine plain dry bread crumbs
2	eggs, beaten
2	tablespoons minced onion
1	teaspoon salt
½	teaspoon ground sage
½	cup ketchup
2	tablespoons packed brown sugar
1	teaspoon dry mustard

1. Combine beef, milk, bread crumbs, eggs, onion, salt and sage in large bowl; shape into loaf. Place meat loaf in **CROCK-POT**® slow cooker. Cover; cook on LOW 5 to 6 hours.

2. Combine ketchup, brown sugar and mustard in small bowl; pour over meat loaf in **CROCK-POT**® slow cooker. Turn **CROCK-POT**® slow cooker to HIGH. Cover; cook on HIGH 15 minutes.

Makes 6 servings

Classic Spaghetti

2	tablespoons olive oil
2	onions, chopped
2	green bell peppers, sliced
2	stalks celery, sliced
4	teaspoons minced garlic
3	pounds ground beef
2	carrots, diced
1	cup sliced mushrooms
1	can (28 ounces) tomato sauce
1	can (28 ounces) stewed tomatoes, undrained
3	cups water
2	tablespoons minced fresh Italian parsley
1	tablespoon sugar
1	tablespoon dried oregano
2	teaspoons salt
2	teaspoons black pepper
1	pound hot cooked spaghetti

1. Heat oil in large skillet over medium-high heat. Add onions, bell peppers, celery and garlic; cook and stir 5 to 7 minutes or until tender. Remove to **CROCK-POT**® slow cooker. Brown beef in same skillet 6 to 8 minutes, stirring to break up meat. Drain fat. Remove to **CROCK-POT**® slow cooker.

2. Add carrots, mushrooms, tomato sauce, tomatoes, water, parsley, sugar, oregano, salt and black pepper to **CROCK-POT**® slow cooker. Cover; cook on LOW 6 to 8 hours or on HIGH 3 to 5 hours. Serve sauce over spaghetti.

Makes 6 to 8 servings

Simple Barbecue Chicken

1	bottle (20 ounces) ketchup
$\frac{2}{3}$	cup packed brown sugar
$\frac{2}{3}$	cup cider vinegar
2	tablespoons chili powder
2	tablespoons tomato paste
1	tablespoon onion powder
2	teaspoons garlic powder
2	teaspoons liquid smoke (optional)
1	teaspoon hot pepper sauce (optional)
8	boneless, skinless chicken breasts (6 ounces *each*)
8	whole wheat rolls

1. Combine ketchup, brown sugar, vinegar, chili powder, tomato paste, onion powder, garlic powder, liquid smoke and hot pepper sauce, if desired, in **CROCK-POT**® slow cooker.

2. Add chicken. Cover; cook on LOW 4 to 6 hours or on HIGH 2 to 3 hours or until chicken is cooked through. Serve with rolls.

Makes 8 servings

Pulled Chicken Sandwiches: Shred the chicken and serve on whole wheat rolls or hamburger buns. Top with mixed greens or coleslaw.

Barbecued Pulled Pork Sandwiches

1	pork shoulder roast (2½ pounds)
1	bottle (14 ounces) barbecue sauce
1	tablespoon lemon juice
1	teaspoon packed brown sugar
1	medium onion, chopped
8	sandwich rolls or hamburger buns

1. Place pork in **CROCK-POT**® slow cooker. Cover; cook on LOW 10 to 12 hours or on HIGH 5 to 6 hours.

2. Remove pork to cutting board; shred with two forks. Discard cooking liquid. Return pork to **CROCK-POT**® slow cooker; add barbecue sauce, lemon juice, brown sugar and onion. Cover; cook on LOW 2 hours or on HIGH 1 hour. Serve pork on rolls.

Makes 8 servings

Tip: For a 5-, 6- or 7-quart **CROCK-POT**® slow cooker, double all ingredients except for the barbecue sauce. Increase the barbecue sauce to 1½ bottles (about 21 ounces total).

Tuna Casserole

8	ounces uncooked egg noodles
2	cans (10¾ ounces *each*) cream of celery soup
2	cans (6 ounces *each*) tuna, drained
1	cup water
2	carrots, chopped
1	small red onion, chopped
¼	teaspoon black pepper
1	egg
	Plain dry bread crumbs
2	tablespoons chopped fresh Italian parsley

1. Prepare noodles according to package directions; rinse and drain.

2. Stir soup, tuna, water, carrots, onion and pepper into **CROCK-POT**® slow cooker. Place whole egg on top. Cover; cook on LOW 4 to 5 hours or on HIGH 1½ to 3 hours.

3. Remove egg; stir in pasta. Cover; cook on HIGH ½ to 1 hour or until onion is tender. Meanwhile, mash egg in small bowl; mix in bread crumbs and parsley. Top casserole with bread crumb mixture.

Makes 6 servings

Note: This recipe does call for a whole raw egg. It will be cooked in the **CROCK-POT**® slow cooker.

Red Beans and Rice

2	cans (about 15 ounces *each*) red beans, undrained
1	can (about 14 ounces) diced tomatoes
½	cup chopped celery
½	cup chopped green bell pepper
½	cup chopped green onions
2	cloves garlic, minced
1	to 2 teaspoons hot pepper sauce
1	teaspoon Worcestershire sauce
1	whole bay leaf
3	cups hot cooked rice

1. Combine beans, tomatoes, celery, bell pepper, green onions, garlic, hot pepper sauce, Worcestershire sauce and bay leaf in **CROCK-POT**® slow cooker; stir to blend. Cover; cook on LOW 4 to 6 hours or on HIGH 2 to 3 hours.

2. Mash bean mixture slightly in **CROCK-POT**® slow cooker with potato masher until mixture thickens. Cover; cook on HIGH ½ to 1 hour. Remove and discard bay leaf. Serve bean mixture over rice.

Makes 6 servings

Black Bean Stuffed Peppers

Nonstick cooking spray
1   medium onion, finely chopped
¼   teaspoon ground red pepper
¼   teaspoon dried oregano
¼   teaspoon ground cumin
¼   teaspoon chili powder
1   can (about 15 ounces) black beans, rinsed and drained
6   large green bell peppers, tops removed
1   cup (4 ounces) shredded Monterey Jack cheese
1   cup tomato salsa
½   cup sour cream

1. Spray medium skillet with cooking spray; heat over medium heat. Add onion; cook and stir 3 to 5 minutes or until golden. Add ground red pepper, oregano, cumin and chili powder; cook and stir 1 minute.

2. Mash half of beans with onion mixture in medium bowl; stir in remaining beans. Spoon black bean mixture into bell peppers; sprinkle with cheese. Pour salsa over cheese. Place bell peppers in **CROCK-POT**® slow cooker.

3. Cover; cook on LOW 6 to 8 hours or on HIGH 3 to 4 hours. Serve with sour cream.

Makes 6 servings

Note: You may increase any of the recipe ingredients except the tomato salsa.

Brownie Bottoms

....

½   cup packed brown sugar

½   cup water

2   tablespoons unsweetened cocoa powder

2½ cups packaged brownie mix

1   package (2¾ ounces) instant chocolate pudding mix

½   cup milk chocolate chips

2   eggs, beaten

3   tablespoons butter or margarine, melted

     Whipped cream or ice cream (optional)

1. Coat inside of **CROCK-POT**® slow cooker with nonstick cooking spray. Combine brown sugar, water and cocoa in small saucepan over medium heat; bring to a boil over medium-high heat.

2. Meanwhile, combine brownie mix, pudding mix, chocolate chips, eggs and butter in medium bowl; stir until well blended. Spread batter in **CROCK-POT**® slow cooker; pour boiling sugar mixture over batter.

3. Cover; cook on HIGH 1½ hours. Turn off heat. Let stand 30 minutes. Serve with whipped cream, if desired.

Makes 6 servings

Banana Nut Bread

⅓ cup butter or margarine

3 ripe bananas, well mashed

⅔ cup sugar

2 eggs, well beaten

2 tablespoons dark corn syrup

1¾ cups all-purpose flour

2 teaspoons baking powder

½ teaspoon salt

¼ teaspoon baking soda

½ cup chopped walnuts

1. Grease and flour inside of **CROCK-POT**® slow cooker. Beat butter in large bowl with electric mixer at medium speed until fluffy. Gradually beat in bananas, sugar, eggs and corn syrup until smooth.

2. Combine flour, baking powder, salt and baking soda in small bowl; stir to blend. Beat flour mixture into banana mixture. Add walnuts; mix thoroughly. Pour batter into **CROCK-POT**® slow cooker.

3. Cover; cook on HIGH 2 to 3 hours. Cool completely; turn bread out onto large serving platter.

Makes 1 loaf

Note: Banana Nut Bread has always been a favorite way to use up those overripe bananas. Not only is it delicious, but it also freezes well for future use.

Super Soups & Stews

Parsnip and Carrot Soup

Nonstick cooking spray

1	**medium leek, thinly sliced**
4	**medium parsnips, chopped**
4	**medium carrots, chopped**
4	**cups chicken broth**
1	**whole bay leaf**
½	**teaspoon salt**
½	**teaspoon black pepper**
½	**cup small pasta, cooked and drained**
1	**cup croutons**
1	**tablespoon chopped fresh Italian parsley**

1. Spray small skillet with cooking spray; heat over medium heat. Add leek; cook 3 to 5 minutes or until golden. Remove to **CROCK-POT**® slow cooker.

2. Add parsnips, carrots, broth, bay leaf, salt and pepper. Cover; cook on LOW 6 to 9 hours or on HIGH 2 to 4 hours or until vegetables are tender. Add pasta during last hour of cooking. Remove and discard bay leaf. Sprinkle each serving evenly with croutons and parsley.

Makes 4 servings

Lentil and Spinach Stew

1	tablespoon olive oil
3	stalks celery, cut into ½-inch pieces
3	medium carrots, cut into ½-inch pieces
1	medium onion, chopped
3	cloves garlic, minced
4	cups vegetable broth
1	can (about 14 ounces) diced tomatoes
1	cup dried brown lentils, rinsed and sorted
2	teaspoons ground cumin
½	teaspoon salt
½	teaspoon dried basil
¼	teaspoon black pepper
5	cups baby spinach
3	cups hot cooked ditalini pasta

1. Coat inside of **CROCK-POT**® slow cooker with nonstick cooking spray. Heat oil in large skillet over medium-high heat. Add celery, carrots, onion and garlic; cook and stir 3 to 4 minutes or until vegetables begin to soften. Remove vegetable mixture to **CROCK-POT**® slow cooker.

2. Stir broth, tomatoes, lentils, cumin, salt, basil and pepper into **CROCK-POT**® slow cooker. Cover; cook on LOW 8 to 9 hours or until lentils are tender. Stir in spinach just before serving. Serve over pasta.

Makes 4 servings

Mediterranean Bean Soup with Orzo and Feta

2   cans (about 14 ounces *each*) vegetable broth

1   can (about 14 ounces) Italian-style diced tomatoes

1   package (10 ounces) frozen mixed vegetables (carrots and peas), thawed

½   cup uncooked orzo pasta

2   teaspoons dried oregano or basil *or* 1 teaspoon *each*

1   can (about 15 ounces) chickpeas, rinsed and drained

½   cup crumbled feta cheese

1. Coat inside of **CROCK-POT**® slow cooker with nonstick cooking spray. Combine broth, tomatoes, mixed vegetables, pasta and oregano in **CROCK-POT**® slow cooker; stir to blend.

2. Cover; cook on LOW 5 to 6 hours or on HIGH 2 to 3 hours. Stir in chickpeas. Cover; cook on HIGH 10 minutes or until heated through. Ladle into shallow bowls; top with cheese.

Makes 6 servings

Simmered Split Pea Soup

3   cans (about 14 ounces *each*) chicken broth

1   package (16 ounces) dried split peas

8   slices bacon, crisp-cooked, chopped and divided

1   onion, chopped

2   carrots, chopped

1   teaspoon black pepper

½   teaspoon dried thyme

1   whole bay leaf

Combine broth, peas, half of bacon, onion, carrots, pepper, thyme and bay leaf in **CROCK-POT**® slow cooker. Cover; cook on LOW 6 to 8 hours. Remove and discard bay leaf. Garnish with remaining half of bacon.

Makes 6 servings

Mediterranean Bean Soup
with Orzo and Feta

Wild Mushroom Beef Stew

1½	to 2 pounds cubed beef stew meat*
2	tablespoons all-purpose flour
½	teaspoon salt
½	teaspoon black pepper
1½	cups beef broth
4	shiitake mushrooms, sliced
2	medium carrots, sliced
2	medium potatoes, diced
1	small white onion, chopped
1	stalk celery, sliced
1	teaspoon paprika
1	clove garlic, minced
1	teaspoon Worcestershire sauce
1	whole bay leaf

*You may double the amount of meat, mushrooms, carrots, potatoes, onion and celery for a 5-, 6- or 7-quart **CROCK-POT**® slow cooker.*

1. Place beef in **CROCK-POT**® slow cooker. Combine flour, salt and pepper in small bowl; sprinkle over meat and toss to coat. Add broth, mushrooms, carrots, potatoes, onion, celery, paprika, garlic, Worcestershire sauce and bay leaf; stir to blend.

2. Cover; cook on LOW 10 to 12 hours or on HIGH 4 to 6 hours. Remove and discard bay leaf.

Makes 5 servings

Note: This classic beef stew is given a twist with the addition of flavorful shiitake mushrooms. If shiitake mushrooms are unavailable in your local grocery store, you can substitute other mushrooms of your choice. For extra punch, add a few dried porcini mushrooms.

Chicken and Sweet Potato Stew

4	boneless, skinless chicken breasts, cut into 1-inch pieces
2	medium sweet potatoes, cubed
2	medium Yukon Gold potatoes, cubed
2	medium carrots, cut into $\frac{1}{2}$-inch slices
1	can (28 ounces) whole stewed tomatoes
1	cup chicken broth
1	teaspoon salt
1	teaspoon paprika
1	teaspoon celery seeds
$\frac{1}{2}$	teaspoon black pepper
$\frac{1}{8}$	teaspoon ground cinnamon
$\frac{1}{8}$	teaspoon ground nutmeg
$\frac{1}{4}$	cup fresh basil, chopped

Combine chicken, sweet potatoes, potatoes, carrots, tomatoes, broth, salt, paprika, celery seeds, pepper, cinnamon and nutmeg in **CROCK-POT**® slow cooker. Cover; cook on LOW 6 to 8 hours or on HIGH 3 to 4 hours. Sprinkle with basil just before serving.

Makes 6 servings

Rich and Hearty Drumstick Soup

2	turkey drumsticks (about 1¾ pounds total)
4½	cups chicken broth
2	medium carrots, sliced
1	medium stalk celery, thinly sliced
1	cup chopped onion
1	teaspoon minced garlic
½	teaspoon poultry seasoning
2	ounces uncooked egg noodles
¼	cup chopped fresh Italian parsley
2	tablespoons butter
¾	teaspoon salt

1. Coat inside of **CROCK-POT**® slow cooker with nonstick cooking spray. Add turkey, broth, carrots, celery, onion, garlic and poultry seasoning. Cover; cook on HIGH 5 hours.

2. Remove turkey to cutting board. Add noodles to **CROCK-POT**® slow cooker. Cover; cook on HIGH 30 minutes or until noodles are tender.

3. Meanwhile, cut turkey into 1-inch pieces; discard bones. Stir turkey, parsley, butter and salt into **CROCK-POT**® slow cooker. Cover; cook on HIGH 10 minutes or until heated through.

Makes 4 servings

Italian Stew

1	can (about 14 ounces) chicken broth
1	can (about 14 ounces) Italian stewed tomatoes with peppers and onions, undrained
1	package (9 ounces) fully cooked spicy chicken sausage, sliced
2	carrots, thinly sliced
2	small zucchini, sliced
1	can (about 15 ounces) Great Northern, cannellini or navy beans, rinsed and drained
2	tablespoons chopped fresh basil (optional)

1. Combine broth, tomatoes, sausage, carrots and zucchini in **CROCK-POT®** slow cooker. Cover; cook on LOW 6 to 7 hours or on HIGH 3 to 4 hours or until vegetables are tender.

2. Stir in beans. Cover; cook on HIGH 10 to 15 minutes or until beans are heated through. Ladle into shallow bowls. Garnish with basil.

Makes 4 servings

Rustic Vegetable Soup

1	jar (16 ounces) picante sauce
1	package (10 ounces) frozen mixed vegetables, thawed
1	package (10 ounces) frozen cut green beans, thawed
1	can (about 10 ounces) condensed beef broth, undiluted
1	to 2 baking potatoes, cut into ½-inch pieces
1	medium green bell pepper, chopped
½	teaspoon sugar
¼	cup finely chopped fresh Italian parsley

Combine picante sauce, mixed vegetables, green beans, broth, potatoes, pepper and sugar in **CROCK-POT®** slow cooker. Cover; cook on LOW 8 hours or on HIGH 4 hours. Stir in parsley just before serving.

Makes 8 servings

Italian Stew

Lentil and Portobello Soup

2	portobello mushrooms (about 8 ounces total)
1	tablespoon olive oil
1	medium onion, chopped
2	medium carrots, cut into ½-inch-thick rounds
2	cloves garlic, minced
1	cup dried lentils, rinsed and sorted
1	can (28 ounces) diced tomatoes
1	can (about 14 ounces) vegetable broth
1	teaspoon dried rosemary
1	whole bay leaf
	Salt and black pepper

1. Remove stems from mushrooms; coarsely chop stems. Cut each cap in half, then cut each half into ½-inch pieces.

2. Heat oil in large skillet over medium heat. Add onion, carrots and garlic; cook and stir 3 to 5 minutes or until onion is tender. Remove to **CROCK-POT**® slow cooker.

3. Place lentils, tomatoes, broth, mushroom caps and stems, rosemary and bay leaf on top. Cover; cook on HIGH 5 to 6 hours or until lentils are tender. Remove and discard bay leaf. Season with salt and pepper.

Makes 6 servings

Tomato Soup with Ditalini

2	cans (28 ounces *each*) whole plum tomatoes
4	cups vegetable broth
1	medium onion, chopped (about 1 cup)
½	medium bulb fennel, chopped (about 1 cup)
2	carrots, chopped (about 1 cup)
3	tablespoons tomato paste
2	tablespoons extra virgin olive oil
3	cloves garlic, minced
1	teaspoon dried basil
1	teaspoon salt
¼	teaspoon black pepper
3	cups hot cooked ditalini pasta
	Grated Parmesan Cheese

1. Coat inside of **CROCK-POT®** slow cooker with nonstick cooking spray. Add tomatoes, broth, onion, fennel, carrots, tomato paste, oil, garlic, basil, salt and pepper; stir to blend.

2. Cover; cook on LOW 7 to 8 hours or on HIGH 3 to 4 hours. Remove soup in batches to food processor or blender; process until smooth. To serve, place ½ cup pasta into each of six bowls and top with soup. Sprinkle with cheese.

Makes 6 servings

Potato Soup

....

8	slices smoked bacon
1	large onion, chopped (about $1\frac{1}{2}$ cups)
2	stalks celery, chopped (about 1 cup)
2	carrots, chopped (about 1 cup)
3	cloves garlic, minced
1	teaspoon dried thyme
5	potatoes (about 3 pounds), cut into $\frac{1}{2}$-inch cubes
4	cups chicken broth
1	cup half-and-half
$\frac{3}{4}$	teaspoon salt
$\frac{1}{4}$	teaspoon black pepper

1. Heat large skillet over medium heat. Add bacon; cook and stir until crisp. Remove to paper towel-lined plate using slotted spoon; crumble. Pour off all but 2 tablespoons bacon fat from skillet and return to medium-high heat. Add onion, celery, carrots, garlic and thyme; cook and stir 5 to 6 minutes or until slightly softened. Stir potatoes, half of bacon and broth into **CROCK-POT**® slow cooker. Cover; cook on LOW 7 to 8 hours or on HIGH 3 to 4 hours.

2. Mash potatoes with potato masher and stir in half-and-half, salt and pepper. Cover; cook on HIGH 15 minutes. Garnish with remaining half of bacon.

Makes 8 servings

Beef Barley Soup

1½	pounds cubed beef stew meat
1	teaspoon salt
½	teaspoon black pepper
5	cups beef broth
2	medium carrots, quartered lengthwise and cut into ½-inch pieces
1	cup chopped onion
1	package (8 ounces) sliced mushrooms
1	leek (white and pale green parts), halved and thinly sliced
2	tablespoons Worcestershire sauce
1	teaspoon soy sauce
1	whole bay leaf
1	cup frozen mixed vegetables, thawed
¾	cup uncooked barley

1. Season beef with salt and pepper. Place beef in **CROCK-POT®** slow cooker. Add broth, carrots, onion, mushrooms, leek, Worcestershire sauce, soy sauce and bay leaf. Cover; cook on LOW 6 hours.

2. Stir in mixed vegetables and barley. Cover; cook on LOW 1 to 2 hours or until barley is cooked through. Remove and discard bay leaf.

Makes 8 servings

Bacon-Mushroom Soup

Nonstick cooking spray

2½ packages (8 ounces *each*) mushrooms, chopped

3 carrots, chopped (about 1½ cups)

2 stalks celery, chopped (about 1 cup)

1 medium onion, chopped (about 1 cup)

2 large shallots, chopped (about ½ cup)

1 teaspoon dried oregano

4 cups beef broth

7 slices bacon, crisp-cooked and chopped, divided

2 tablespoons tomato paste

2 tablespoons soy sauce

¼ teaspoon black pepper

1. Spray large skillet with cooking spray; heat over medium-high heat. Add mushrooms; cook and stir 3 to 4 minutes or until softened. Stir in carrots, celery, onion, shallots and oregano; cook 2 minutes. Remove mushroom mixture to **CROCK-POT**® slow cooker using slotted spoon. Stir in broth, 5 tablespoons bacon, tomato paste and soy sauce.

2. Cover; cook on LOW 6 to 7 hours or on HIGH 3 to 3½ hours or until vegetables are tender. Remove 4 cups soup to food processor or blender; process until smooth. Return to **CROCK-POT**® slow cooker; stir in pepper. Top with remaining 2 tablespoons bacon.

Makes 6 to 8 servings

Easy Entertaining

Nacho Dip

1	**tablespoon vegetable oil**
1	**onion, chopped**
2	**pounds ground beef**
2	**cans (about 15 ounces** *each***) black beans, rinsed and drained**
1	**can (28 ounces) diced tomatoes**
1	**can (about 15 ounces) refried beans**
1	**can (about 15 ounces) cream-style corn**
3	**cloves garlic, minced**
1	**package (1 ounce) taco seasoning**
	Tortilla chips
	Queso blanco

1. Heat oil in large skillet over medium-high heat. Add onion; cook 2 to 3 minutes or until translucent. Add beef; brown 6 to 8 minutes, stirring to break up meat. Drain fat.

2. Stir beef mixture, black beans, tomatoes, refried beans, corn, garlic and taco seasoning into **CROCK-POT**® slow cooker. Cover; cook on LOW 5 to 6 hours or on HIGH 2½ to 3 hours. Serve beef mixture on tortilla chips; sprinkle with queso blanco.

Makes 10 cups

Holiday Ham

1	bone-in cooked ham (about 5 to 7 pounds), trimmed
16	whole cloves
1	cup water
1½	teaspoons vegetable oil
1	shallot, chopped
1	jar (12 ounces) cherry preserves or currant jelly
¾	cup dried orange-flavored cranberries or raisins
½	cup packed brown sugar
½	cup orange juice
½	teaspoon dry mustard

1. Score ham. Place 1 clove in center of each diamond. Pour water into **CROCK-POT**® slow cooker; add ham. Cover; cook on LOW 5 to 6 hours or on HIGH 2½ to 3 hours or until ham is heated through.

2. Heat oil in small saucepan over medium-high heat. Add shallot; cook and stir 2 to 3 minutes or until translucent. Stir in preserves, cranberries, brown sugar, orange juice and dry mustard. Reduce heat to medium; cook until sugar is dissolved.

3. Remove ham from **CROCK-POT**® slow cooker; drain liquid. Return ham to **CROCK-POT**® slow cooker; pour perserve mixture over ham. Cover; cook on HIGH 10 to 20 minutes or until fruit plumps.

Makes 12 to 14 servings

Creamy Artichoke-Parmesan Dip

- 1 teaspoon olive oil
- 2 tablespoons finely chopped onion
- ½ can (about 7 ounces) artichoke hearts, drained and chopped
- ½ cup half-and-half
- ½ cup (about 2 ounces) mozzarella cheese
- ⅓ cup grated Parmesan cheese
- ⅓ cup mayonnaise
- ⅛ teaspoon oregano
- ⅛ teaspoon garlic powder
- 4 pita bread rounds, toasted and cut into wedges

1. Heat oil in medium saucepan over medium heat. Add onion; cook and stir 3 to 5 minutes or until tender. Add artichoke hearts, half-and-half, cheeses, mayonnaise, oregano and garlic powder; cook and stir until mixture comes to a boil.

2. Coat inside of **CROCK-POT® LITTLE DIPPER®** slow cooker with nonstick cooking spray. Fill with warm dip. Serve with pita wedges.

Makes 1½ cups

Party Meatballs

- 1 package (about 1 pound) frozen cocktail-size turkey or beef meatballs
- ½ cup maple syrup
- 1 jar (12 ounces) chili sauce
- 1 jar (12 ounces) grape jelly

Place meatballs, syrup, chili sauce and jelly in **CROCK-POT®** slow cooker; stir to blend. Cover; cook on LOW 3 to 4 hours or on HIGH 2 to 3 hours.

Makes 10 to 12 servings

Creamy Artichoke-Parmesan Dip

Tropical Chicken Wings

1	jar (12 ounces) pineapple preserves
½	cup soy sauce
½	cup chopped green onions
3	tablespoons lime juice
2	tablespoons pomegranate molasses or honey
1	tablespoon minced garlic
2	teaspoons spicy chili sauce
¼	teaspoon ground allspice
3	pounds chicken wings, tips removed and split at joints
1	tablespoon toasted sesame seeds*

To toast sesame seeds, spread in small skillet. Shake skillet over medium heat 2 minutes or until seeds begin to pop or turn golden brown.

Combine preserves, soy sauce, green onions, lime juice, molasses, garlic, chili sauce and allspice in **CROCK-POT**® slow cooker; stir to blend. Add wings to sauce; toss to coat. Cover; cook on LOW 3 to 4 hours or until wings are cooked through. Sprinkle with sesame seeds just before serving.

Makes 6 to 8 servings

Tip: Pomegranate molasses is a syrup made from pomegranate juice cooked with sugar. You can easily make your own if it isn't in the ethnic foods aisle of your local supermarket. For this recipe, bring to a boil ½ cup pomegranate juice, 2 tablespoons sugar and 1 teaspoon lemon juice in a small saucepan over medium-high heat. Cook and stir until reduced to about 2 tablespoons.

Pork Roast with Spicy Orange Glaze and Black Beans

1	boneless pork loin roast (3 pounds)*
1	teaspoon salt
½	teaspoon black pepper
1	onion, chopped
2	cloves garlic, finely chopped
1	can (about 14 ounces) chopped tomatoes
2	cans (about 15 ounces *each*) black beans, rinsed and drained
¼	cup orange marmalade
¼	teaspoon ground red pepper

*Unless you have a 5-, 6- or 7-quart **CROCK-POT**® slow cooker, cut any roast larger than 2½ pounds in half so it cooks completely.*

1. Season pork with salt and black pepper. Heat large nonstick skillet over medium-high heat. Add pork; cook 6 to 8 minutes or until browned on all sides. Remove to **CROCK-POT**® slow cooker.

2. Add onion to same skillet; cook and stir 2 to 3 minutes or until just beginning to brown. Add garlic; cook 30 seconds. Add tomatoes, stirring to scrape up any browned bits. Pour over pork.

3. Pour beans around pork. Cover; cook on HIGH 1¾ hours or until roast reaches 140°F. Remove roast to cutting board. Cover loosely with foil; let stand 10 to 15 minutes. Melt marmalade in small saucepan over medium heat. Stir in ground red pepper; brush over roast. Slice pork and serve with bean mixture.

Makes 10 servings

Spiced Beer Fondue

2	tablespoons butter
2	tablespoons all-purpose flour
1	can (8 ounces) light-colored beer, such as ale or lager
½	cup half-and-half
1	cup (4 ounces) shredded smoked gouda cheese
2	teaspoons coarse grain mustard
1	teaspoon Worcestershire sauce
⅛	teaspoon salt
⅛	teaspoon ground red pepper
	Dash ground nutmeg (optional)
	Apple slices and cooked potato wedges

1. Melt butter in medium saucepan over medium heat. Sprinkle with flour; whisk until smooth. Stir in beer and half-and-half until mixture comes to a boil. Cook and stir 2 minutes. Stir in cheese, mustard, Worcestershire sauce, salt and ground red pepper; cook and stir until cheese is melted.

2. Coat inside of **CROCK-POT® LITTLE DIPPER®** slow cooker with nonstick cooking spray. Fill with warm fondue. Sprinkle with nutmeg, if desired, and serve with apples and potatoes.

Makes 1½ cups

Herbed Artichoke Chicken

1½ pounds boneless, skinless chicken breasts

1 can (14 ounces) artichoke hearts in water, drained

1 can (about 14 ounces) diced tomatoes, drained

1 small onion, chopped

1 cup chicken broth

½ cup kalamata olives, pitted and sliced

¼ cup dry white wine

3 tablespoons quick-cooking tapioca

1 tablespoon chopped fresh Italian parsley

2 teaspoons curry powder

1 teaspoon dried sweet basil

1 teaspoon dried thyme

½ teaspoon salt

½ teaspoon black pepper

Combine chicken, artichokes, tomatoes, onion, broth, olives, wine, tapioca, parsley, curry powder, basil, thyme, salt and pepper in **CROCK-POT**® slow cooker; mix well. Cover; cook on LOW 6 to 8 hours or on HIGH 3½ to 4 hours or until chicken is cooked through.

Makes 6 servings

Tip: For a 5-, 6- or 7-quart **CROCK-POT**® slow cooker, double all ingredients, except for the chicken broth and white wine. Increase the chicken broth and white wine by one half.

Mango Spiced Ribs

2	tablespoons vegetable oil
3	pounds beef short ribs
1	cup mango chutney
1	teaspoon curry powder
1	clove garlic, minced
½	teaspoon salt
½	teaspoon ground cinnamon

1. Heat oil in large skillet over medium heat. Add ribs; cook 5 to 7 minutes or until browned on all sides.

2. Combine chutney, curry powder, garlic, salt and cinnamon in medium bowl; rub mixture onto ribs. Place in **CROCK-POT**® slow cooker. Drizzle remaining chutney mixture over ribs. Cover; cook on LOW 6 to 8 hours or on HIGH 3 to 4 hours.

Makes 6 servings

Feta and Mint Spread

- ½ cup plain Greek yogurt
- 3 ounces feta cheese, crumbled
- 2 ounces cream cheese, cubed
- 2 tablespoons extra virgin olive oil
- 1 small clove garlic, crushed to a paste
- 1 tablespoon chopped fresh mint
- ½ teaspoon grated fresh lemon peel
   Baked Pita Chips (recipe follows)
   Carrot and celery sticks

1. Butter inside of **CROCK-POT® LITTLE DIPPER®** slow cooker. Add yogurt, feta cheese, cream cheese, oil and garlic; mix well. Cover; heat 1 hour or until cheese is melted.

2. Meanwhile, prepare Baked Pita Chips.

3. Stir in mint and lemon peel. Serve with Baked Pita Chips, carrot and celery sticks.

Makes 12 servings

Baked Pita Chips

- 3 pita bread rounds
- 1 tablespoon extra virgin olive oil
- ½ teaspoon dried oregano
- ¼ teaspoon ground cumin
- ⅛ teaspoon salt

1. Preheat oven to 375°F. Spray large baking sheet with nonstick cooking spray.

2. Brush one side of each pita round with oil. Sprinkle with oregano, cumin and salt. Cut each pita round into 12 wedges. Place on prepared baking sheet seasoned side up. Bake 8 minutes or until lightly browned.

Makes 36 chips

Pears with Apricot-Ginger Sauce

¼ **cup water**

4 **whole firm pears (about 2 pounds total), peeled with stems attached**

1 **tablespoon lemon juice**

2 **tablespoons apricot fruit spread**

1 **teaspoon grated fresh ginger**

½ **teaspoon cornstarch**

½ **teaspoon vanilla**

1. Coat inside of **CROCK-POT**® slow cooker with nonstick cooking spray. Add water. Arrange pears stem side up. Spoon lemon juice over pears. Cover; cook on HIGH 2½ hours. Remove pears; set aside.

2. Combine fruit spread, ginger, cornstarch and vanilla in small bowl; stir until cornstarch dissolves. Whisk mixture into water in **CROCK-POT**® slow cooker until blended. Cover; cook on HIGH 15 minutes or until sauce thickens slightly. Spoon sauce over pears.

Makes 4 servings

Bananas Foster

12	bananas, cut into quarters
1	cup flaked coconut
1	cup dark corn syrup
2/3	cup butter, melted
1/4	cup lemon juice
2	teaspoons grated lemon peel
2	teaspoons rum
1	teaspoon ground cinnamon
1/2	teaspoon salt
12	slices pound cake
1	quart vanilla ice cream

Combine bananas and coconut in **CROCK-POT**® slow cooker. Stir corn syrup, butter, lemon juice, lemon peel, rum, cinnamon and salt in medium bowl; pour over bananas. Cover; cook on LOW 1 to 2 hours. To serve, arrange bananas on pound cake slices. Top with ice cream and warm sauce.

Makes 12 servings

Recipe Index

Metric Conversion Chart

VOLUME MEASUREMENTS (dry)

$1/8$ teaspoon = 0.5 mL
$1/4$ teaspoon = 1 mL
$1/2$ teaspoon = 2 mL
$3/4$ teaspoon = 4 mL
1 teaspoon = 5 mL
1 tablespoon = 15 mL
2 tablespoons = 30 mL
$1/4$ cup = 60 mL
$1/3$ cup = 75 mL
$1/2$ cup = 125 mL
$2/3$ cup = 150 mL
$3/4$ cup = 175 mL
1 cup = 250 mL
2 cups = 1 pint = 500 mL
3 cups = 750 mL
4 cups = 1 quart = 1 L

VOLUME MEASUREMENTS (fluid)

1 fluid ounce (2 tablespoons) = 30 mL
4 fluid ounces ($1/2$ cup) = 125 mL
8 fluid ounces (1 cup) = 250 mL
12 fluid ounces ($1 1/2$ cups) = 375 mL
16 fluid ounces (2 cups) = 500 mL

WEIGHTS (mass)

$1/2$ ounce = 15 g
1 ounce = 30 g
3 ounces = 90 g
4 ounces = 120 g
8 ounces = 225 g
10 ounces = 285 g
12 ounces = 360 g
16 ounces = 1 pound = 450 g

DIMENSIONS

$1/16$ inch = 2 mm
$1/8$ inch = 3 mm
$1/4$ inch = 6 mm
$1/2$ inch = 1.5 cm
$3/4$ inch = 2 cm
1 inch = 2.5 cm

OVEN TEMPERATURES

250°F = 120°C
275°F = 140°C
300°F = 150°C
325°F = 160°C
350°F = 180°C
375°F = 190°C
400°F = 200°C
425°F = 220°C
450°F = 230°C

BAKING PAN AND DISH EQUIVALENTS

Utensil	Size in Inches	Size in Centimeters	Volume	Metric Volume
Baking or Cake Pan (square or rectangular)	8×8×2	20×20×5	8 cups	2 L
	9×9×2	23×23×5	10 cups	2.5 L
	13×9×2	33×23×5	12 cups	3 L
Loaf Pan	8½×4½×2½	21×11×6	6 cups	1.5 L
	9×9×3	23×13×7	8 cups	2 L
Round Layer Cake Pan	8×1½	20×4	4 cups	1 L
	9×1½	23×4	5 cups	1.25 L
Pie Plate	8×1½	20×4	4 cups	1 L
	9×1½	23×4	5 cups	1.25 L
Baking Dish or Casserole			1 quart/4 cups	1 L
			1½ quart/6 cups	1.5 L
			2 quart/8 cups	2 L
			3 quart/12 cups	3 L